Look at what they're saying about

THE LITTLEST STAR
A Parable

"A story you will treasure and want to share."
—The Rev. Joan L. Carter

"A simple but powerful way to teach values and open doors to new possibilities."
—Doug Yeaman, Author The Power Of Commitment

"This story will help millions of children realize that they are stars too."
—Jack Canfield, Co-Author, Chicken Soup for the Soul

"The child in all of us will respond to this warm, wonderful, uplifting and inspiring story."
—Richard Paul Evans, Author The Christmas Box

"A story in the true spirit of Christmas, and destined to become for thousands, what it has already become for our family, a holiday tradition."
—Kate Harper, Motivational Speaker

StarRight Publishing

Sausalito, CA 94965

THE LITTLEST STAR
A Parable

by David K. Tanner

THE LITTLEST STAR, A PARABLE

PRINTING HISTORY
Limited Paperback edition / Dec 1994

Illustrations by Lenny Hanlock
Cover Design by Deon Staffelbach

For information address:
StarRight Publishing.
3020 Bridgeway, Sausalito, CA 94965

ISBN 0-9642798-0-0

PRINTED IN THE UNITED STATES OF AMERICA

ACKNOWLEDGMENTS

This book is the result of a three year struggle: challenges, hurdles, trials, and disappointments—all of my own creation. The road has also been filled with inspiration, generosity, friendship, and joy.

While it is well-nigh impossible to mention all the names of those people who have assisted me and made this book possible; I do, however, especially wish to acknowledge the following:

My parents, who filled a house with love and were an example of living one's principles.

My religious upbringing, which taught me spiritual and eternal truths.

My friends, those who were there for me like Buzz, Rob, Doug, Charlie, Mike, Ted and Kathleen; and for those who weren't.

The literary agents and publishers who refused to take on the project—this made me stronger and more determined.

To Publishers Distribution Center, who saw the vision.

To the "Dream-stealers" who helped me in spite of themselves.

To a tough cowboy named Frank, who gave and gave; just because I asked and he could.

To Simon and Schuster for allowing me to use the quotes from *Running and Being* by George A. Sheehan, M.D.

Special thanks for the generous financial assistance from Presley and Stacey Reed.

He telleth the number
of the stars,
he calleth them all
by their names.

— Psalms 147:4

To Jeff, Bob and Meredith, my special stars,
and to the unique star qualities in all of us.

Once upon a time...

In the vastness of the Milky Way
Where stellar lights adorn,
Before Earth was formed
or time began,
A little star was born.

The old Star Keeper noted,
In the ancient Star Lore Book,
The birth of this faint little light,
That most might overlook.

It was called The Littlest Star,
Because of its small size,
But great were all the goals
and dreams
It hoped to realize.

This starchild had a winning smile
Across its small star face,
And filled with curiosity
Through heavens it would race.

"I want to grow up big and bright,
To make my parents proud.
I'll be a member of some team,
And rise above the crowd."

But, because it was so tiny,
        The big star kids poked fun.
It couldn't join in any games,
        No, not a single one.

So sitting sadly all alone
        It thought, "They tease me now,
But I'll show them what I can do;
        And that's my solemn vow!"

"I've heard of the giant Rigel,
        The biggest star I know.
I'll ask how he became so big;
        Then I will grow and GROW!"

"It is frightening to leave home
        And travel the unknown,
But if my desire is strong enough
        The answers will be shown."

The Littlest Star journeyed long
Through dark unfriendly space,
Till it found Rigel large and fat,
Conceit upon his face.

Trembling with fear,
the small star spoke,
"Please, I don't mean to pry,
But tell me how you got so big.
Then I'll give it a try."

The giant glared down at the runt
And laughed, "Ha, Ha, Ho, Ho!"
You're no bigger than a planet.
You'll never be big, NOW GO!"

The little star was shaken,
Upset and feeling sad.
When an optimistic thought
occurred,
"It's no use getting mad."

"He may think he's important,
But he's star wrong not star right.
I came to him for answers, and
He wouldn't share his light."

“The brightest star is Sirius.
I’ll find her and I’ll ask
How she radiates so brightly?
Then I’ll take on the task.”

Bright Sirius was beautiful,
But, Oh! so proud and vain,
She looked down on the little star
With nothing but disdain.

“You will never match my brilliance,
If that’s your foolish aim!”
Then scorchingly, she singed the star
With her sharp tongue of flame.

Wiping away the sooty spots,
        "She's star wrong not star right.
Inside she's dull and empty;
        Only outwardly she's bright."

"Their conceit and self-importance
        Have caused me such frustration.
Maybe I'll join a star group,
        A stellar constellation."

So searching space, it found the bull,
The constellation Taurus,
Who's silver horns shook as he spoke,
"Get lost, you're not for us!"

"You're dull and insignificant.
You'd never fit in right.
Just look at the way you sparkle;
You're not our kind of light."

In anger, Taurus pawed stardust.
His Bull's-eye flared bright red.
A snort like thunder spun the star
Cartwheeling on its head.

Still dizzy and dismayed it thought,
"He's star wrong not star right.
Just because I'm small and different,
That's no reason for such spite."

Then feeling lost and all alone,
It began to sob, "Boo Hoo!
I can't seem to find my answers;
Oh what am I to do?"

With eyes full of tears,
it failed to see
Dark danger there lurking.
The dream-stealer of the universe
Lying in wait smirking.

Suddenly, this Black Hole Monster
Seized the small star and then
Twirled it, swirled it,
whirled it around—
Again, Again, Again.

Black, black, blackness everywhere,
        The star cried a frantic prayer,
"Oh Star Keeper please help me now;
        Save me from this nightmare!"

A cold icy grip muffled the prayer,
        The starchild's last word.
Its light became faint...
                        flickered...
                                out.

...But the prayer had been heard!

Instantly, in starburst splendor,
        The Star Keeper appeared.
Its white light so magnificent;
        The Black Hole disappeared.

As the small star looked around, it
        Realized it was kneeling.
Overwhelmed by love and light,
        But at peace with this feeling.

In a tiny timid voice, it spoke.
"Oh Star Keeper, please tell me;
Can I become a super star?
That's what I'd like to be."

The Star Keeper spoke lovingly,
"My friend, you must commit.
Your stardom quest has just begun,
And you must never quit."

"Beware of all the dream-stealers
Who tell you that you can't.
They feed on negativity,
They put down, rave and rant."

"Your life has a special purpose;
Things only you can do.
Each star is different, quite unique,
So enjoy being you."

"I will leave you with this counsel,
Because I have heard your plea.
Remember who YOU are, and then,
Be the best YOU can be!"

The Star Keeper then vanished and
The reverie was broken.
Leaving the small star to ponder
Those truths which had been spoken.

"From this moment, it's up to me
To build life bit by bit.
I'll pursue my life's real mission,
And never, ever, quit!"

"I don't need to seem important,
Or admired from afar.
I'll just remember to be me;
Cause I was born a star!"

As eons of time passed slowly,
The small star was heard to say,
"I will shine brighter and brighter,
In my own special way."

So fulfilling its destiny,
Brighter and brighter it blazed.
Its dazzling light like diamonds,
The other stars were amazed.

Then one dark, silent, Holy night,
Three wise men on a quest
Were guided by a promised star,
Brighter than all the rest.

Shining high over a stable,
        Lo, exceeding great joy!
Born this day in Bethlehem,
        A wondrous, Holy Boy.

Glory to God in the highest!
        Peace, good will toward all.
A multitude of angels sang
        Above the humble stall.

Now every year at Yuletide,
        Look closely, you will see,
Twinkling at the tippy top
        Of a tall, green, Christmas tree,

        The Littlest Star.

A shining symbol for our times,
Reminding you and me.
Dreams can come true.
Reach for the stars.

BE THE BEST YOU CAN BE!

If thou follow thy star, thou canst not fail of a glorious haven.

—Dante, *The Inferno of the Divine Comedy*
Canto XV (1321)

AFTER-WORDS

REACH FOR A STAR

The early morning sun lit the placid water of the mountain lake creating a giant reflecting pool. Towering redwood trees and rocky cliffs nose-dived into the blue-green water making an exact color copy of the trees, rocks, and sky above.

Running at the feet of these shaggy barked giants, on trails littered with their castoffs, was always inspiring, but today was special. Today, I would receive a gift.

I know that may seem overly dramatic, but, even though this experience happened nearly three years ago, I still thrill at the memory of those brief moments–my run around Phoenix Lake, the creative bursts, and the flood of words transcribed on my tape recorder as I ran. The Littlest Star and the advice, "Be The Best You Can Be", were born in that hour by the lake.

From his book *Running and Being,* Dr. George Sheehan describes, in his own inimitable way, how I felt about my experience at that moment of inspiration:

"There, in a lightning flash, I can see truth apprehended whole without thought or reason. There I experience the sudden understanding that comes unmasked, unbidden."

My desire in including these few pages is to show that dreams can come true; however, there is always a price tag. Also, this price, no matter what it may be, is worth it when you follow your higher or spiritual purpose.

When the story of The Littlest Star first came to me on that morning run, I decided it would make an ideal motivational story for a sales organization I headed at the time, so I subtitled it, *A Parable.* Webster defines parable as, "A short story designed to convey a truth or moral lesson." It has the same Greek root as the word parallel, meaning side by side or similar course. People can relate similarities of the story to events in their own lives.

As I pursued my dream of publishing, *The Littlest Star, A Parable* , I began to notice the parallels of my own life compared with the experiences of the title character.

Similar to the little star, I had big dreams. In my case, it was publishing a book that could have a positive impact on people. I encountered a Rigel like person. He was an investment banker. In short order, he dismissed my ideas with a supercilious smugness.

While attending The American Booksellers Association convention in Los Angeles, I sought help for my book project. I was introduced to a woman similar to Sirius. She gloried in her position as the chief buyer for one of the largest book distributing firms in the country. She was rude and had no time for me. Her angry words seared not only me, but the poor salesman that was doing me the favor of an introduction. I left feeling verbally "scorched".

My appointment with a famous publisher reminded me of the constellation Taurus episode. I was shown in no uncertain terms why my book did not meet their criteria. It would, "never fit in right...You're not our kind of light."

Finally, I became embroiled with "dream-stealers". This involvement with a group of investors became a "Black Hole" that threatened to annihilate any chances of publishing *The Littlest Star, A Parable*. They attempted to steal the project with their superior financial resources.

Like the tiny hero being sucked into oblivion, as a last hope, I turned to prayer. In my case, not to the ancient Star Keeper, but to the star Creator; God the Eternal Father, "who created all things by Jesus Christ," Ephesians 3:9.

The fact that this little book is in your hands at this moment in time is proof that prayers are answered and dreams can come true. All you need is a passionate desire, belief that it can happen, and then take the necessary action.

The mind keeps us from doing things it doesn't believe are possible, but once it accepts the belief that it can do something, chances are good we will be able to do it. Once you believe you can, you can. The Bible puts it succinctly, "If thou canst believe, all things are possible to him that believeth," Mark 9:23.

This book is the result of a life process. Different challenges are faced by each of us on our unique journeys to "stardom". Mine included being broke, in debt, homeless, without a car, and often relying on friends and family members to get by.

Throughout this personal three year "soap opera", I was armed with the power of "my dream". The basic truth is: to do anything, you must first believe it can be done, and that it can be done by you. Secondly, take appropriate action. Belief releases creative powers. Disbelief puts the brakes on. When you believe, your mind finds the means to achieve the result you believe in; but you must take action. Action is belief in motion.

It has been said, "We judge others by their actions; yet we would be judged by our intentions." The Bible says, "...by works was faith made perfect," James 2:22. If you will excuse my paraphrase, By action is desire and belief made perfect.

We are defined by our actions. It is our actions that speak volumes about our real being. A wise man once said, "It is our conduct—towards ourselves and toward the outside world—which will truly tell us who we are. All else is merely self-deception."

The old Star Keeper's advice, "Be The Best You Can Be", implies action. Often, for me, action equates to running. Running is transformational for me. Faced with a problem or a challenge, I will go for a run; not to run away from the problem, but to run towards a solution. Running is creative; running is "moving meditation"

The point I would like to make here is: "Move". Don't stay stuck. Some direction is better than "no" direction. When we get off the couch and out the door, we are greeted with new vistas, new vantage points and new possibilities.

The process of believing in and publishing *The Littlest Star, A Parable* has brought me rich rewards that money can't buy. I have found good and generous friends, loving support from family, a new personal testimony of Jesus Christ, and reservoirs of personal strength and endurance that come from desire, belief, prayer and the ability to put it all in motion through action.

This book is a simple little story with a big message. I would pray that The Littlest Star might be a bright symbol of hope and a call to action—at a time when, for many people, hope is in short supply and action is required.

The Littlest Star came unbidden as a gift to me, and I pass it along in that same spirit.

Even so faith, if it hath not works, is dead, being alone.
...For as the body without the spirit is dead, so faith without works is dead also.

—James 2:17,26

Climb High.
Climb Far.
Your Goal The Sky,
Your Aim The Star.

—Anonymous

AUTHOR

David K. Tanner has taught motivation and self-actualization to thousands of independent sales distributors. David is an avid runner, and it was during one of his morning runs that the inspiration for The Littlest Star came to him. While competing in over thirty marathons around the world, including London, Paris, New York, and Boston, he realized that it was not as important to win as to be the best he could be.

He has also competed six times in the Ironman Triathlon at Kona, Hawaii, where he was an age group winner. This is his first book.

One star differeth from
another star in glory.

—1 Corinthians 15:41

What you are is
God's gift to you...
What you make of yourself
is your gift to God.

—Old Proverb

We Would Like To Hear From You!

You can help us all reach for the stars. If you have been touched by this book, or if you have a personal story of beating the odds and overcoming major setbacks in search of your dream, or if you have a favorite story you have read; we would like you to share this with us.

If we can use any of the material in any future volume, we will make sure that you and/or the author are credited for the contribution. Thank you.
Please send to:

StarRight Publishing
3020 Bridgeway
Suite 162
Sausalito, CA 94965
(415) 905-8877